MILLION DOLLAR PRODUCTIVITY

To Ray —

MILLION DOLLAR PRODUCTIVITY

Write Faster!

Kevin J. Anderson

WordFire Press
Colorado Springs, Colorado

MILLION DOLLAR PRODUCTIVITY
Copyright © August 2014 WordFire, Inc.

The authors and publisher have strived to be as accurate and complete as possible in creating the Million Dollar Writing series. We don't believe in magical outcomes from our advice. We do believe in hard work and helping others. The advice in our Million Dollar Writing series is intended to offer new tools and approaches to writing. We make no guarantees about any individual's ability to get results or earn money with our ideas, information, tools or strategies. We do want to help by giving great content, direction and strategies to move writers forward faster. Nothing in this book is a promise or guarantee of future book sales or earnings. Any numbers referenced in this series are estimates or projections, and should not be considered exact, actual or as a promise of potential earnings. All numbers are for the purpose of illustration. The sole purpose of these materials is to educate and entertain. Any perceived slights to specific organizations or individuals are unintentional. The publisher and authors are not engaged in rendering legal, accounting, financial, or other professional services. If legal or expert assistance is required, the services of a competent professional should be sought.

ISBN: 978-1-61475-229-5

Cover design by Janet McDonald
and
Art Director Kevin J. Anderson

Cover artwork images by Dollar Photo Club

Book Design by RuneWright, LLC
www.RuneWright.com

Published by
WordFire Press, an imprint of
WordFire, Inc.
PO Box 1840
Monument CO 80132

Kevin J. Anderson & Rebecca Moesta, Publishers

WordFire Press Trade Paperback Edition August 2014
Printed in the USA
wordfirepress.com

THE MILLION DOLLAR WRITING SERIES

When seeking advice, always consider the source. Many self-appointed "experts" write how-to books without themselves ever accomplishing the thing they are trying to teach you how to do.

In the Million Dollar Writing Series, each of our authors has sold a minimum of one million dollars of commercial product in their field. They have proved themselves, and here they share their wisdom, advice, and experience with you.

There are many factors in becoming a successful writer, and we cannot guarantee that you'll break into the top levels, but we hope you find the advice to be useful and enlightening.

CONTENTS

INTRODUCTION

Back in the heyday of pulp fiction magazines, when freelancers struggled to pay the bills by writing stories for half a cent per word (at most), they had to produce, produce, produce. Their motto was "Be prolific or starve." Armed only with manual typewriters and carbon paper, the most popular and productive writers managed to crank out entire novels in only a few days, stories and novelettes in a single sitting.

Today, with an arsenal of writing tools that includes word processors, email, scanners, internet research, lightning-fast printers, digital recorders, and voice-recognition software, it must be easy for modern authors to be even more prolific than their "prehistoric" predecessors. Right?

Life is crazy and hectic for most of us. We're surrounded with personal and family obligations, jobs, fitness programs, virtual mountains of email, not to mention videogames, TV, smartphones, social networking, and millions of things to check out on the web.

With all those distractions, how does an aspiring author find time to write?

And when you do find the time, how do you make the most of it?

That's what I'll show with this book. You don't have to be manically productive (though some of us consider that to be fun), but you will learn ways to get more writing out of every available moment.

PART I

No Excuses — Finding the Time to Write

Being a Full-Time Writer

I'm not a typical writer, I admit that. I might be at the far end of the bell curve regarding the time and energy I spend on writing. This is a conversation that runs through my head:

Writing isn't a hobby. Writing is a passion.

Writing is a way of life.

Writing is the thing that comes to mind first when you ask yourself, "What am I doing today?"

Writing is always in the back of your mind— when you're watching football games with the family, or sitting in a meeting at work, or waiting to be served at a restaurant, or fidgeting in the dentist's office. The voice inside keeps whispering louder and louder, "I could be *writing* right now!"

When you glimpse interesting people in a crowd, when you experience an unusual event, when you see a spectacular landscape, your immediate reaction is, "How can I use this in my writing?"

If those statements ring true—if you smile and say, "Hey, that's me!"—then this book is for you.*

Standard disclaimer: There's nothing wrong with dabbling, either. It's enjoyable and often therapeutic to unleash your creative impulse. Don't worry if you can't write all the time—you'll still find parts of Million Dollar Productivity *useful.*

Comic writer/artist Howard Tayler says, "Being a full-time writer is great. You only have to work half days—and you get to decide which twelve hours that is."

I am a full-time writer, 24/7—birthdays and holidays included, 365 days a year. Most of my full-time writer friends have a similar schedule. They center their lives around researching, writing, editing, publishing, and promoting what they write. It's not an easy job.

What does it mean to be a writer, one hundred percent? Every aspect of life has something to do with writing, or how you can apply it to your writing. It's how you frame the things you do in a way that they have some bearing on writing. Obsessive? Okay, maybe a little.

I have written adult books, non-fiction, young adult books, even children's pop-up books. I have worked in the fields of science fiction, fantasy, mainstream thrillers, mysteries, horror, comedy, urban fantasy, even historicals. I have done comic books, articles, short stories, and novels so thick that whole forests tremble when my publisher contacts the printing plant for the first press run.

I have been a waiter in a restaurant, a bartender, a caretaker for white lab rats used in medical research, a farm worker, a technical writer and editor, and a co-owner of a beauty salon. I love to climb mountains or hike long wilderness trails.

I am the co-producer on a major film, as well as a public speaker, a workshop presenter, a published photographer, a graphic designer, a record producer, president of a small company, and with my wife Rebecca Moesta, the publisher of WordFire Press.

So far.

And I generally write five or more novels a year. I've learned how to get the most out of every possible minute I have available to write, and I'll share some of the techniques I've learned.

If Only I Had the Time

During the Olympics, the world watches great athletes from all nations perform seemingly impossible feats. When those well-toned men and women receive their medals, we admire them for their almost superhuman abilities.

As we sit on the couch munching potato chips, however, most of us don't kid ourselves that we would be just as skilled, just as fast, just as strong … if only we had the time.

But for some reason, a lot of people believe that about *writing books*. Anyone can write, they say. How hard can it be to string a bunch of sentences together? They could do it if they just sat down and put their minds to it. If only they had the time.

Here's how the conversation often goes:

A person at one of my book-signings or appearances walks up to the table, shuffles feet, looks away, then looks at me. "I've always wanted to be a writer. I could write a novel."

Me: "Oh? Why haven't you?"

Person: "I just don't have the time."

Me: "Hmm. Can't you scrape together a few hours a week to devote to the project?"

Person: "No. I'm really busy."

Me: "You know, nobody gives me the time, either. I have to *make* the time, set priorities, discipline myself to write each day, no matter how tired I am. I worked a full-time regular job while I wrote my first novels, jealously stealing an hour here or there in the evenings and on weekends. That's how I became a successful author."

Person: "Well, you're lucky then. I just don't have that kind of time."

Olympic athletes usually start their training as kids, practicing, competing, working their way up year after year. Some of them get up before dawn just to squeeze in enough hours of training during the day. They strive to improve their performance, stretch their abilities, beat their personal bests, and then beat them again. They practice until they're ready to drop, but they keep at it. Many end up injured along the way. The vast majority of those who try out for the Olympic team don't make it. They may win semifinals and regional competetions, but only the best of the best become part of the Olympic team—and only the very best of those will win a medal.

I've received dozens of letters posing the same question: "I want to write a bestselling novel. But it takes so long, and it's an awful lot of work. What's the shortcut?"

Does anyone really say, "I want to win a gold medal in figure skating, but I don't have the time for all that practice and training. In fact, I don't even own ice skates. Can you tell me the shortcut to winning a medal?"

Without doing a full comparison, I wouldn't be surprised if there are about as many *New York Times* bestselling authors as there are members of the various U.S. Olympic teams. The competition among bestsellers is just as tough, and your chances of success are just as slim.

You try your best. You fail. You try again. You fail. You try harder, you get better. You still fail. You keep trying, keep getting better, keep getting battered. Failure becomes a routine, and you don't let it bother you. Trying and trying again becomes an obsession. And finally, maybe, something works.

I got my first rejection slip at the age of thirteen, had my first story published when I was sixteen (after I had gathered eighty rejection slips), and sold my first novel by the time I was 25.

No, I don't know any shortcuts. Sorry. But I can tell you some mistakes to avoid.

Where does this notion come from that *anybody* can write a novel, if they just get around to it? I never hear the claim that just anybody can be a brain surgeon, or a space shuttle commander, or the manager of a business empire. Even if we did "have the time" to raise capital and invest wisely, few people could succeed in becoming as rich as Warren Buffett.

But to the unpracticed eye, publishing a novel involves little more than stringing a lot of sentences together until you fill enough pages with words.

Every author has heard this suggestion from a friend or a fan, and the proposition never ceases to amaze me: "I've got a great idea for a novel. I'll tell you the idea, you write the book, and then we can split the money." (As if the *idea* is the hard part!) In all honesty, I always have plenty of ideas. In fact, I'll never have time to flesh out all the novel possibilities that occur to me on a regular basis.

I've often wished I had the nerve to reply: "Why don't we try it the other way around first? I'll tell *you* an idea off the top of my head, then you do all the research, the plotting, and character development. You can write a hundred thousand words or so, then edit the manuscript (I usually do at least five to ten drafts), sell it to the publisher, work with the editor for any revisions, deal with the copy editor, proofread the galleys, then do booksignings and promotion after it's published. Then, after all that, we'll split the money. Sound fair?"

Now, I'm not comparing myself to an Olympic gold medalist. I can't even stay up on ice skates. I don't change the oil in my car, remodel the bathroom, or put in my own landscaping, though I could probably figure it out, "if only I had the time." But I do have a solid grasp on how to write a novel. I've been practicing and training for most of my life.

You just have to make the time.

No Excuses

When I was in college taking creative writing courses, I fell in with a "writer's group" that met on campus every Thursday afternoon. I knew I wanted to be a writer, and I thought hanging around with other aspiring authors would be a great way to get inspiration and make connections.

The best-laid plans ...

This group of wannabees would sit in a local coffee house all afternoon, through dinner, and far into the night, sipping cappuccino or mineral water as they talked about the great novels they intended to publish someday.

And hour after hour, they bemoaned the fact that they never had enough time to write.

After listening to their complaints, I figured out a miracle solution to the problem—I stopped going to their kaffeeklatsch and spent those hours writing instead. It was amazing how productive I could be when I actually devoted my time to *writing* instead of *talking about writing*.

No excuses.

You never just HAVE time to write.

You need to MAKE time to write.

Last week I was in Hollywood for the Writers of the Future awards and workshop, where my wife and I teach. Because we had obligations—

attending rehearsals, teaching classes, as well as taking several business meetings while in LA (you know, movie producers, comic company executives, potential collaborators on multimedia projects, and even just seeing old friends)—my writing time was sparse and frequently interrupted.

I had brought along notes and a (too-optimistic) list of projects I hoped to complete during the trip. In particular, I needed to write the introduction to an anthology I'm editing and also do the full proposal for a new Dune novel with Brian Herbert that my agent and publisher were waiting for. Because of the chaotic schedule, I had to take advantage of snippets of time, and I needed to focus when I did have the chance.

An anthology introduction is relatively simple to write, but you need to have something to *say*. During downtime (while going to sleep, for instance, or while in the shower) I mulled over what I wanted to include in the intro—a beginning, middle, end ... in essence, a *point*. The whole thing would be only three pages or so; it wouldn't take me long to write—I just had to find a few minutes here and there.

No excuses. It needed to be done.

There was a Starbucks in the shopping mall across the street from our hotel, and I would get coffee for Rebecca and me every morning, maybe a refill late in the morning, maybe another hot drink in the afternoon. The walk was five or ten minutes each way, each time. Not much, but those were minutes I would otherwise have wasted. In fact, it was enough time to dictate a page or so into my recorder on each trip. (I usually write my first drafts by dictating while I walk—more on that later in the book.)

And I got the intro done in a day.

The proposal for the Dune novel was a lot more involved. Brian Herbert and I had already brainstormed the plot, and I had all my notes. I needed the time, space, and concentration to get a coherent summary down on paper.

During the workshop that day, I had an hour or two between my times in front of the class, so I found a quiet, private place to use my laptop. I closed the door, sat down, put my earphones on, and started writing the "movie trailer" version of the novel Brian and I had plotted—typing a few paragraphs at a time of a plotline or a major scene. Each time I had a break, I could get several sections done before I was called back to duty.

In the afternoon, I found another hour, closed the door again, wrote some more scenes, summarized another storyline. Later that night, after dinner and socializing with some of the students, I was getting ready for bed … but the incomplete proposal weighed on me. It was still unfinished. I had only the climactic sections to write.

No excuses.

So I sat down at the hotel room desk and kept myself awake for another hour, causing much more fictional mayhem, and finished fleshing out the grand finale of the novel. I had written the entire book proposal in the odd hour here and there during other duties throughout the day. When I was done, those snippets had added up to eight completed manuscript pages.

Not bad for a day's work *full time*, yet I had managed to do it in otherwise wasted minutes.

With so much else going on during the Hollywood trip, I could have made excuses and let those minutes or hours trickle away unnoticed. Instead, I wrung out an introduction and a book proposal.

You can do it, too. What's your excuse?

A Day at Work

Early in my career, a well-respected science fiction writer asked if I would collaborate with him on a short story. At the time, he was at the height of his career, winner of numerous awards, a *New York Times* bestseller. I couldn't figure out why he would want to collaborate with a relative newbie like me. He answered, "To learn how you can be so prolific."

After we had worked together for a few months, he had his answer. "OK, I now know

15

how you produce so much—it's because you write *all the time!*"

Everyone else has to put in a day at work—typically eight hours on the job, five days a week (more if there's overtime).

As a full-time writer, expect to put in just as much time "at work" as anyone else who has a challenging full-time job.

A teacher is expected to be at school before the buses arrive, to teach classes all day, to stay until after the students have gone, and to grade papers into the night. A doctor sees patients all day long, usually eight hours or more. A lawyer spends the entire day writing briefs, researching cases, meeting with clients, filing papers, appearing in court.

Granted, I love to be writing—in fact, I'm even a little obsessive about it—so I like putting in time at my career. But even when people don't like their jobs, they still have to go to work and put in their hours in order to earn a paycheck. I wouldn't guess that sanitation engineers or snowplow drivers love their jobs, but they still go to work. It's expected of them.

At the World Science Fiction Convention many years ago, I was on a panel with award-winning author Octavia Butler and bestselling (and also award-winning) author Dr. Jerry Pournelle. Octavia asked for advice on how to deal with writer's block, and Jerry responded with his signature curmudgeonliness. "There's an easy cure for writer's block. You just sit down and write one sentence, then write the next one, then write the next one. No more writer's block."

Alarmed, Octavia asked, "But what if it's not any good?"

Jerry just blinked. "Well, then you fix it!"

Do bank tellers or librarians get to stay home and wait for the muse to "inspire" them before they go to work? Nope.

Does a mail carrier say, "I think I have 'postal delivery block,' and I just can't do my route today"? Nope.

Does a surgeon cancel his scheduled procedures for the day because she doesn't feel "inspired" to perform a hernia operation? Does a barista stay home because he just doesn't feel the creative satisfaction of making coffee that day?

Why shouldn't a writer do a full day of work— as in actually writing for hours? Put in your time. Butt in chair, fingers on the keyboard, producing words.

A Typical Frantic Schedule

Due to a series of unfortunate commitments, travel schedules, and other book obligations, I found myself facing a tough deadline for the first book in a new trilogy set in my popular Saga of Seven Suns universe: *The Dark Between the Stars*. I had been planning the novel for a year, but there was always some emergency, some crunch proofing deadline, some quick project that took precedence. So I didn't get around to starting when I thought I would.

Besides, when facing a manuscript that would be close to a thousand pages long, it was easy to procrastinate.

I had been thinking about *The Dark Between the Stars* for a long time, but I'd been away from the Seven Suns universe for more than five years, and so I had to reread all seven volumes, take notes, and re-load all of those details into my head. I worked on developing character sketches, fleshing out how the fictional situation had changed in twenty years since the end of the previous series.

For months, I worked on the plot, pouring out ideas, juggling them to see which storylines fell into Book 1, which ones fit better in Book 2. I wrote a very detailed chapter-by-chapter outline (itself over a hundred pages long), a full-fledged blueprint with a paragraph or two summarizing each of the book's 130 chapters.

All of this was prep work, like a race car revving its engine, building up power, just waiting for the start light to turn green. When I had my full outline in hand, I was ready to go.

Since the draft manuscript was due to my editors in January, I needed to get writing! On October 1, armed with my detailed outline, a reasonably clear schedule, and a *lot* of coffee, I yelled "Banzai!" (metaphorically) and dove in.

Back in 2000, when I began to write *Hidden Empire*, the first volume in the Saga of Seven Suns, I went to hike a nice local trail leading up to the Palmer Lake Reservoirs; on the trail that day, armed with my microcassette recorder, I had written the first three chapters.

Hoping to recapture that magic, I did the same this time. With my notes in hand for the first few chapters in *The Dark Between the Stars*, I hit the Reservoir trail, digital recorder in hand (technology upgrade). I was ready to go, with 130 chapters ahead of me.

I'd had the novel's first sentence in my head for months. "He had to run, and he fled with the boy out into the dark spaces between the stars." From that point, all I needed to do was write the next sentence. And the next. On that day's hike, surrounded by mountains and under clear blue skies, I wrote the first four chapters. I was off and running.

126 more chapters to go.

Each day, I would set out in the morning to do a minimum of two chapters (approximately 2,000 words each). Sometimes in the afternoon I'd go out again and write another one or two. During this marathon, my maximum was six chapters in a day, or about 12,000 words. After each session, I emailed the digital audio files to my typing service. During my most intense pace, I kept three typists busy nearly full time just to process my output.

Every day another two chapters, or three, or more.

But I was interrupted for three days to go to Toronto as a guest speaker at RushCon and then attend the Rush Clockwork Angels concert at the Toronto Air Canada Center. Then another three days in Fargo, ND, where my wife Rebecca and I were guests of honor for ValleyCon, then a five day trip to LA for Disneyland (Rebecca's birthday), the Anaheim Rush Clockwork Angels concert, a book signing in Burbank at Dark Delicacies, and various meetings with friends. Then up to Denver one evening for a Vertical Horizon concert.

(Even if I write all the time, I do occasionally have a real life, too.)

Then back to writing to make up for lost time.

As a counterpoint to all those distracting appearances and commitments, I carved out a few days to go out to Capitol Reef National Park in Utah, where I hiked in the canyons and dictated enough chapters to get back on schedule again. I dictated new material day by day and, when transcribed chapters came back from the typists, I would try (and fail) to keep up with a first edit.

Exhausting, yes. But there was an advantage, too. The sheer fact of being so immersed in the world, the characters, and the intricate plot of *The Dark Between the Stars* gave me a heightened sense of focus, a momentum that kept me rolling along at full speed. I didn't want to do anything else, just get back to those gigantic cosmic problems, throw my characters into traumatic situations, and save them (or maybe not).

Another looming distraction stood in my way, however: on December 2, Rebecca and I had to be instructors on the Sail to Success Caribbean writing cruise. I most certainly did NOT want to be derailed from my daily writing just as I was approaching the big finale! So I decided to finish before we started the cruise.

I pushed harder, wrote an extra chapter per day ... and finished the final piece, chapter 130, with four days to spare.

220,000 words in 47 writing days, 900 pages ... which I then had to edit, while letting my brain rest and recharge for the next project.

Which I started two weeks later.

A More Typical Day

Now, the *Dark Between the Stars* schedule was crazy even for me. I don't (can't) do that level of intensity all the time. But I've always been a very productive writer, and I tend to put in a full work week.

Here's a more typical day—not that there is ever a truly typical day.

❖

Alarm goes off at 6:45 AM. Listen to the news, have coffee, make breakfast, do a 45-minute workout in the gym (usually while listening to an audiobook, with a notepad nearby in case any ideas spring to mind).

9:30 A.M. Read and answer email, work on social media. Then study chapter notes and get set up for the day.

10:00 A.M. Head out to a local trail or bike path and dictate two chapters while hiking. Rain or shine, snow or wind.

Lunch at home, often as a brainstorming or business meeting with Rebecca.

Afternoon: Edit chapters received from the typist, make business phone calls, proofread galleys, work on outlines, or do research for future projects.

5 P.M. Cook dinner (I like cooking, and we work hard enough to deserve a good meal)—usually while listening to the news or an audiobook.

Evening: Watch TV shows (usually genre shows, which are research for possible projects), while using my laptop to answer emails and post to social media outlets; time permitting, write a blog or answer emails, answer interview questions for magazines or websites.

Before bed, I relax in a hot bath where I have time to read (although the reading usually turns out to be work-related, not pleasure reading, such as manuscripts for an anthology I'm editing, or proofing my own galleys).

Around midnight, Rebecca and I go to bed.

Next day starts the same, seven days a week ... except for the numerous business trips, trade shows, conventions, and other obligations.

That's a day at work, a fairly average one—a lot of hours spent on one aspect of writing or another, and I usually manage to be quite productive. But before I pat myself on the back too much, realize that such a schedule isn't much different from the workday of, say, a corporate executive, the owner of a busy restaurant, or a hospital administrator.

This is my job. This is my career. This is how I make a living. And like anyone else who has a freelance occupation, if I don't do work, I don't get paid. If I don't deliver what I promised, I'm not likely to get another contract with that publisher.

A professional writer treats a day at work like a day on the job.

It's the difference between a career and a hobby.

PART II

THE MATHEMATICS OF PRODUCTIVITY

Literary elitists often frown on prolific authors. A productive writer, they say, can't possibly put in the proper amount of hours and effort to create a worthy book. Only through prolonged time and muse contemplation can one possibly produce a decent novel.

Or so they claim.

The reality is, it's virtually impossible for anybody who writes only one book per year to make a living at it, to pay the mortgage, the grocery and electric bills, the insurance, the kids' college funds.

Now, that's fine if you have a nice day job with benefits, and you're content to earn your income doing something else while you dabble in writing for personal satisfaction whenever the muse hits you.

But if you want to *support yourself* by writing, if you want to *Be A Writer*, you're going to have to be productive. It's a numbers game.

Over my twenty-five years as a novelist, I've published more than 120 books—about five a year, on average. I write, and publish, 300,000–500,000 words annually.

Now, some snobs roll their eyes because of their ingrained—but completely *wrong*—assumption that "high productivity equals poor quality."

How do you measure quality?

My novels have received numerous starred reviews in major magazines and have been included on several "Best of the Year" lists. To date 53 of my books have hit national or international bestseller lists, including 21 on the *New York Times* list. My novels have won or been nominated for most of the major awards in my field—the Nebula Award, Bram Stoker Award, SFX Reader's Choice Award, the Faust Lifetime Achievement Award, Science Fiction Book Club Reader's Award, Romance Writers of America RITA Award, Private Eye Writers Association Shamus Award, American Physics Society's Forum Award, *New York Times* Notable Book, and more.

Whatever your measure, *something* in there should denote a reasonable level of quality.

And I routinely write five books a year.

Some of the greatest writers in literature wrote quickly—many of them in longhand (even with goose quills!). Alexandre Dumas, Jules Verne, and Charles Dickens were amazingly prolific, and their works have remained on bookshelves for centuries.

According to *Wired* Magazine (Jan 2012), Charles Dickens wrote *A Christmas Carol*, one of the best-loved novels of all time, in a feverish frenzy that lasted about six weeks. In longhand.

William Faulkner wrote his classic *As I Lay Dying* also in six weeks and claimed to have published his first draft "without changing a word."

Anthony Burgess wrote *A Clockwork Orange* in three weeks.

Jack Kerouac wrote *On the Road* in twenty days, supposedly on a single continuous roll of paper.

Ray Bradbury wrote his classic *Fahrenheit 451* in nine days—on a rental typewriter at UCLA, plunking in a dime for every hour of use.

Robert Louis Stevenson wrote *The Strange Case of Dr. Jekyll & Mr. Hyde* in *one week*.

So … why must high productivity indicate poor quality? Let's just dispense with that myth, shall we? Fast writing does not mean BAD writing … any more than slow writing equals good writing. A writer can spend years and years and still produce a mediocre book.

What other industry or trade actually *frowns upon* hard work and productivity? Imagine a carpenter receiving *complaints* from a customer because he worked twelve hours a day for two weeks, seven days a week, to meet a promised deadline.

Or how about a factory worker being *reprimanded* because he produces more than his coworkers? Or an accountant who balances the books and finishes the tax forms well ahead of schedule?

For some reason, though, literary elitists complain when a writer produces "too many books" (as determined by some arbitrary scale)— as if ideas and stories are somehow in short supply in a good writer's imagination.

They don't understand the mathematics of productivity.

Authors who write one book a year—which many "gatekeepers" of literature consider an "acceptable" level of productivity—almost certainly cannot support themselves by writing alone. Therefore, they have to work another full-time job to pay the bills. I've talked with many such authors and noted their writing schedules.

Between work and personal obligations, that person might manage an hour or two of writing in the evenings, some during the weekends. All told, it adds up to maybe ten hours per week of actual writing.

Therefore, by simple math, over the course of a year, the writer with a full-time day job might spend approximately 520 hours writing and editing a novel. Apparently, that's the right amount of time to devote to a "good" novel, according to the literati.

520 hours.

Okay, let's go with that.

Full-time writers, on the other hand, can work all day long, and all week long, on writing and editing. And they usually do.

For my own part, as I described in the previous section, I put in 8–10 hours a day, usually seven days a week. That's 56 hours of writing per week, on average.

Do the math. Even at a conservative estimate, I can devote the requisite 520 hours to producing a novel manuscript—the "acceptable" amount of time a writer should spend on a book (see above)— in eleven weeks.

Run the numbers again if you need to. Eleven weeks.

At that rate, with the "right" amount of time and effort on a novel, I will produce five or six books per year.

In other words, a full-time writer who devotes the same number of hours to a writing career as, say, a dedicated restaurant owner devotes to running a restaurant, can write *five books a year*, spending 520 hours writing and editing each one.

As a matter of fact, that has been my average output over the course of my career as a novelist.

Slow writing ≠ good writing.

Fast writing ≠ bad writing.

Are you a good writer, or not?

Yes, the literary elitists who see an author's byline on too many book covers over the course of a year are quick to dismiss those novels as rushed or sloppy, when in fact the author may well have spent as many hours—or more—on each manuscript as a typical one-book-per-year, part-time writer does.

It's just simple mathematics.

PART III

KEVIN'S ELEVEN — 11 TIPS TO INCREASE YOUR WRITING PRODUCTIVITY

By this point, I hope you're convinced you want to be more productive. Good job. That's fine in theory.

But *how* do you increase your productivity? What techniques do you use to squeeze more hours, more words, more concentration time out of every single day?

From my own experience, as well as from discussions with other prolific writers, I've compiled the following eleven tips to help you go a bit longer or wring out a few more words each time you write.

These suggestions aren't applicable to every situation—in fact, some are even contradictory—

but try the techniques and see if some of them work for you. It's a toolbox for productivity.

Writing Productivity Tip #1
Shut Up and Write!

A writer's muse is usually depicted as an ethereal woman with a gentle voice whispering hints and ideas that might eventually find their way into a story. Right? We all know the stereotype of writers who don't do much more than sit around, mulling over esoterica, occasionally jotting down a phrase or two when the muse inspires them. One brilliant metaphor, and that's enough for the day, right? What more can you expect?

I, on the other hand, have been blessed (or cursed) with a muse who's more like a bristle-haired, gravel-voiced drill sergeant who says, "Quit dinking around, Anderson! Sit down, shut up, and WRITE!" No puttering, no procrastinating. Butt in chair, fingers on keyboard, eyeballs on screen.

Shut up and write!

If writing is a priority for you, then writing should *take priority* over reading the morning paper, sharing joke emails, talking to a friend on the phone, watching game shows on TV, going to a movie, making scrapbooks of last year's family vacation, playing with the cats (or dogs, or fish, as your particular case may be), cleaning the kitchen, or going shopping. The other stuff can wait until you get your pages done.

If you don't believe that, then writing isn't your **priority**.

❖

Writers are among the only people in the world who would rather be cleaning the bathroom than doing their job. When you do get a spare moment to write, whether it's late at night, at lunch, or early in the morning, don't find excuses and waste time for "just one little thing."

Procrastination is the writer's deadliest enemy. Learn how to spot when you're finding excuses instead of writing. Or—to use a technical term—*dinking around*.

To reiterate the instructions of my drill-sergeant muse:

Butt in chair
Fingers on keyboard.
Eyeballs on screen.

If this means keeping a regular draconian writing schedule, do it—and make sure that you *write* during those times (i.e., "produce words that line up into sentences that are stacked in paragraphs," rather than mulling over a metaphor that might one day be used in a poem). Don't merely stare out the window like a kid on a rainy day—*get to work*.

Everybody else has to go to a job and put in their time. (See earlier section about doctors, lawyers, teachers, and sanitation engineers.) If you aim to be a professional writer, then do your job.

Shut up and write.

Be tough on yourself and on the people around you. Make sure that your chatty friends know that you are not to be disturbed during your writing time. "Sorry, I can't talk right now. This is my work day." Just like a teacher. Just like a doctor. Just like anyone else with a full-time job. Turn off the ringer on the phone if you need to and let voicemail do what it's designed to do.

If you don't take your own work seriously, you can't expect others to.

Writing Productivity Tip #2
Defy the Empty Page

In any project, the most difficult sentence to type is often the first one. With a 500-page novel looming ahead of you—or even a fifteen-page short story—getting started can be like trying to push a semi truck uphill with two fingers (your typing fingers).

Staring at the empty page or blank screen is an intimidating experience, but if you can trick yourself into typing that first word, and then the first sentence, followed by the first paragraph—you'll start the whole story rolling.

Defy the empty page. Don't let the blank screen psych you out.

In the movie *Throw Momma from the Train*—a writer's movie if there ever was one!—the writer character played by Billy Crystal spends hours producing mounds of torn and crumpled sheets of paper as he strives to complete his precious first sentence.

"The night was ..."

Hour after hour, he gets no farther than that. His agonizing struggle for inspiration provides great laughs as he paces the floor and stares at his typewriter. He thinks he's got to get the first sentence absolutely perfect before he moves on to the second sentence. After all, didn't Mark Twain claim that the "difference between the right word and *almost* the right word is the difference between lightning and a lightning bug"?

No one will ever be struck by your literary "lightning," however, if you never finish the book!

And you can't finish until you get started.

Struggling to get your first sentence down can be a silly, but serious, hang-up. The first sentence has to be a hook, the all-important line that captures our reader.

BUT worrying overmuch about getting it *Just Right* can cause creative paralysis to set in. You must start your fingers typing, or your pen writing, or your recorder recording.

And the first step is to start with *something*.

Here's an idea: If the "perfect first sentence" eludes you, then write the *second* sentence or the next paragraph—get going on the next step *after* the perfect first sentence and start telling your story. Just get the words moving. As you really sink into your scene, you'll be more in tune with what makes the best opening line. Then you can come back and add it afterward.

If starting your new project still seems intimidating, then do something to get the fingers warmed up and your mind in gear. Some writers start by retyping the page where they left off the last session, or even just a random paragraph out of a nearby book, simply as a mechanical exercise to get your fingers and brain moving.

It doesn't matter, so long as you start writing.

Once the page isn't empty anymore, you're over that psychological speed bump.

And before you know it, you're off and running.

Writing Productivity Tip #3
Work on Different Projects at the Same Time

This tip works best for people with ADD or low boredom thresholds, and it doesn't work for everybody, but it has helped me maintain a high productivity level through all stages of many books and stories.

From start to finish, a writing project has many phases: research, plotting, writing, multiple edits, then copyedits, proofreading, and finally the marketing and business side of publication.

And some of these tasks are more onerous than others.

To help even out the hard parts with the fun parts, I keep several different projects in different stages on the creative burner at all times. I can switch from one, to another, to another, and always keep moving forward.

Personally, I love plotting the story from scratch as well as writing the first draft. It's like a fun creative explosion. But the first major edit after I've written the draft, or the last proofread after I've read a novel a dozen times—those seem like drudgery.

If I have several novels or stories at different stages of completion, however, I can *switch* from one process to another. When I get exhausted from one type of work, I can change gears and charge along at full-steam in a different direction.

The simultaneous variety also makes the tedious parts more palatable, the proverbial medicine taken with a spoonful of sugar analogy. I spend an hour researching a new novel, then write a draft chapter of a different story, then proofread galleys of another novel, answer questions in an interview for yet another project, then maybe go back to tweak an outline, or get back to doing more research.

Okay, I admit I'm a restless Type-A person, hopscotching among projects like a guy with a TV remote bouncing from channel to channel. But this method keeps me fully productive at all times.

In the few weeks before originally writing this section, I worked my way through the first rough edit of *The Sisterhood of Dune*, input Rebecca's detailed copy edits to *The Key to Creation*, did the final proofread of the typeset galleys for *Star Challengers #2: Space Station Crisis*, plotted and wrote a proposal for "The Saga of Shadows," read short story submissions for my anthology *Blood Lite 3*, worked out details for promotion and a book-signing tour for *Hellhole Awakening*, wrote and posted several blogs, and did logistical planning for our next Superstars Writing Seminar.

All of these things got juggled into the daily writing schedule, and I switched from one, to the next, to the next, always keeping my brain moving.

I find that after working on the same project for a while, it begins to lose its freshness and becomes more tedious. And when I'm not enjoying myself, the process of writing becomes a chore instead of a joy. I try not to let that happen, because I *love* writing. When I grow weary of one type of work (say, the drudgery of proofreading) I can reward myself with doing something else (the enjoyable process of outlining or first-draft writing, for instance), and still keep "writing."

So far, I haven't gotten any of my stories mixed up.

Writing Productivity Tip #4
Dare to Be Bad (at First) … Then Fix It

Repeat after me: It doesn't have to be perfect, but it does have to be *finished*.

It's easier to FIX existing prose than it is to write perfect prose in the first place. The crucial step is to *get it down on paper*.

Don't get too obsessive the first time around. Your draft words or descriptions might be redundant. So what? They can be fixed later.

You might make grammatical mistakes. So what? Promise yourself you'll take care of it *after* you've got the story written. Get it down on paper. No one publishes a "perfect" but only half-completed novel.

A few years ago, I wrote my award-winning, #1 bestselling X-Files novel ***Ground Zero*** in six weeks, start-to-finish: 300 published pages, 90,000 words. The publisher had already scheduled it for a breakneck production pace, and everyone was counting on me to deliver the manuscript. I could not be late. I absolutely, positively had to turn in an acceptable novel on time.

The only way I could accomplish this was just to tell my story, get it down on the page, and trust in my writing skills. See the previous section, "A Day at Work."

I managed to write 25–30 pages a day on that book, seven days a week, until the draft was finished. Although this isn't an exercise I recommend for most writers, the sheer, intense concentration did increase my writing speed and, I believe, my writing quality as well. By writing straight through, one scene after another without wandering back to earlier chapters to tweak the prose, I built up a "story momentum" that propelled the book along at a breakneck pace.

As soon as the first draft of *Ground Zero* was done, I allocated as much time as possible to polish the words, and I edited the manuscript again and again until the last second.

Surprisingly, when I went back to the initial pages, fully intending to spend weeks on major rewriting, I discovered that the constant, intense practice had taught me to produce crisp, fast-paced writing as compelling as if I'd spent hours agonizing over each page.

Remember, you can always go back and make changes—always. If you let self-doubt (or the lack of the "perfect" word or phrase) keep you from moving on to the next sentence, then you'll never finish that paragraph—which means you'll never finish that chapter, which means you'll never finish that novel.

Giving yourself permission to "be bad, then fix it" frees your mind just to create. For the first draft, don't worry about how good it is or how you can revise it. Just do the writing.

Writing Productivity Tip #5
Use Every Minute

How many of you have all the writing time you could possibly want?

Sure, we'd all love extended, uninterrupted hours to do nothing but sit and ponder, to write page after page while immersed in the story and characters without a distraction in the world … but that's a luxury most of us don't have.

If you think you can only use large blocks of time to accomplish writing, you're kidding yourself. One sentence at a time, one paragraph at a time, one page at a time.

In the real world, the majority of writers—even successful, published writers—still have full-time jobs and need to squeeze in their writing around other duties. Writers have families, obligations, even—surprise!—personal lives.

I didn't actually quit my day job until I'd published eleven bestsellers. It was a 40+ hour per week position with heavy responsibilities, involving frequent travel, as well as constant pressures and distractions. Even so, by taking advantage of snippets of time in the evenings and on weekends, and a spare lunch hour or two, I managed to write two or three novels per year. With a full-time job.

If you have only a few minutes here and there, then learn how to *do something productive* in those brief bursts.

You can plot a short story in the shower, develop a character background while waiting in the dentist's office, map out a scene before drifting off to sleep at night. Make progress—however small—on your project during the five or ten minutes in the theater before the movie starts, while cooking dinner, or while doing tedious household tasks. While riding the bus or vanpool, you can write down notes, scribble outlines, even mark up a printout of an earlier chapter.

Those few minutes here and there add up.

Too often I've heard the lame excuse, "I don't have enough time to do a serious amount of writing, so I'll just *[insert procrastinating activity]* instead." Science fiction writer Roger Zelazny used to advise authors to "write two sentences."

Two sentences. Not such an insurmountable obstacle.

You may really only have time to write two sentences; in other instances, though, those two sentences might lead to two more sentences, and then two paragraphs. Ten minutes later, you'll have a page done.

A free ten minutes is **ten minutes you could be writing**. Two sentences will take you two sentences closer to finishing the manuscript.

If you find yourself in a place where you really can't jot down detailed notes (say, in the gym or waiting in line at the grocery store) use every little snatch of time to ponder **what** you're going to write the next time you get a few minutes at your keyboard. Do your mulling ahead of time, so that when you do have a few spare moments to sit with your butt in the chair and your fingers on the keys, you can jump right in and get down to actual writing instead of pondering what you mean to say.

When you have a longer chunk of time to write—an hour, part of an afternoon, a day off—use it to WRITE! Get as much written as you can. This takes a lot of discipline, and it's easy to get distracted, but set your priorities.

Do you want to be a writer? Then *be* one. Write.

Writing Productivity Tip #6
Set Goals for Yourself … and Stick to Them

I'm a goal-oriented person. Give me a target, or a list, and I'll set out to accomplish the task, milestone by milestone.

When I moved to Colorado, I got a book that listed all of the state's 54 mountain peaks higher than 14,000 feet, along with hiking or climbing routes to each summit. Now there was a worthy goal for an ambitious hiker! I immediately made up my mind to climb every last one of them—and I did, over the course of the next several years.

Similarly, when you set yourself a writing objective, you give yourself a target to shoot for—and therefore you have a greater chance of achieving it. You can measure the goal in different ways—set aside *one hour* per day of dedicated writing, or produce *four pages* a day, or finish a new story each month.

If you find yourself making too many excuses, try a clear-cut goal to keep yourself accountable.

A caution: Know yourself well enough to set *realistic* targets, rather than ridiculous ones. If you repeatedly fail to meet your goals, you'll get discouraged.

Once you learn how to meet your goal of 1,000 words per day, for example, then up the stakes to 1,500 words a day. Push yourself.

A regular writer's group may provide you with that incentive, such as having to complete a story before the next meeting. Join (or form) a support/competition group that sets goals for their members (e.g., each member must submit a piece of writing at each meeting for the other group members to critique).

Instead of creating undue pressure, the friendly competition can be mutual support among your fellow writers.

The members of a highly successful group in Oregon regularly engage in competitions among themselves. In "the Race," they compete with one another, keeping track of who has the most submissions in the mail at any one time. The loser buys the others dinner.

But no one is the loser, really, because even the person with the lowest output is more productive than he or she would have been without the inspiration of those fellow writers.

Try entering writing contests; you can find many of them listed online. All of these contests have deadlines that force you to complete your entry by a certain date. In the science fiction and fantasy field, one particularly successful contest is the Writers of the Future; it's been around for more than three decades, and Rebecca and I are both judges, along with many of the most respected writers in the genre. We highly recommend it.

The prospect of winning, as well as a set deadline for entries, may give you the nudge you need.

*(**Caution**: Beware of contests that claim all publication rights to submissions. Don't give up your story, no matter how good the contest sounds.)*

Each November is National Novel Writing Month, during which entrants pledge to complete a 50,000-word novel manuscript in 30 days. In the most recent year's Nanowrimo, participants produced 2.8 ***billion*** words in a single month. Even if you don't think you're ready for a challenge of that magnitude, follow next November's Nanowrimo and get inspired.

Writing Productivity Tip #7
Know the Difference Between WRITING and EDITING

Write during the writing stage.

Edit during the editing stage.

Even though both activities involve sitting at the keyboard (usually) and staring at the screen, *Writing* and *Editing* are two very different processes. Each requires a separate set of skills and talents. One taps the creative side of your brain, and the other taps the analytical side. Learn to recognize the difference, and teach yourself to focus on only one process at a time.

Writing is the creative part of the process. When you're writing—creating—let yourself get caught up in your story and be swept away by the characters, setting, and situation as the plot unfolds. (See Tip #4.) Don't worry about the commas. Write the story first: Tell what happens, where it happens, and who it happens to, without fiddling with the previous paragraph, polishing one bit of dialogue, rearranging the sentences, researching subtle rules of usage, looking up historical dates, or finding the proper punctuation. That will just hang you up and stall the writing. No need to get every spelling or grammar guideline correct at this stage. You'll have ample opportunity to do that later.

Once the creative part is done, when your draft is written and the story told, *then* activate the analytical part of your brain. Change hats and become an ***Editor*** instead of a ***Writer***.

Okay, now is your opportunity to look at the sentence structure, cull out the redundant phrases, correct the grammar, add the appropriate punctuation, run your spell check, look up Napoleon's birthdate, double check the color of your character's eyes.

As I'll describe in Tip #9, I have two totally separate methods for writing and editing. I do my initial drafts by dictation while I hike. This is an advantage, since it's not physically possible for me to worry about, or even see, cosmetic nuances of grammar or punctuation. After I dictate the first draft and have it transcribed, then I do my editing on the computer.

I've seen too many writers derail their creative process by stopping the action to tweak a word or a sentence. If you write a few paragraphs, then go back and polish them, you destroy all the forward momentum you had. It's like shifting gears— forward, reverse, forward, reverse. You could burn out your mental transmission.

If you can train yourself to save the criticism for the second draft, you'll actually finish writing and have something to polish.

Create the Best Writing Environment
for Yourself

So, you've developed a writing routine, set up an office or at least a place where you do your writing, and you've gotten accustomed to it. Why bother changing, if it works?

But sheer habit doesn't necessarily make your setup beneficial to your writing. Just because you've been using a certain place at a certain time in a certain way, doesn't mean that's the *only* way you can be productive. Have you ever stepped back with an objective eye to consider whether it *works best* for you?

Is your "office," whether it's a spare bedroom, a corner of the kitchen table, or an old desk in the garage, really conducive to the most productivity? Don't just accept whatever work environment happened to coalesce around you as you started writing. Consider other possible rooms, desks, tables in the house. Try to create a "haven" for yourself, a place that you can call a writing office, so that when you're working there, you—and everyone else—regard it as your real workplace.

Look at where you have your computer or laptop set up. Is it on a TV tray in the middle of the living room with chaos and clutter all around? Probably not the best spot. Is it a corner of the kitchen table with any old chair pulled up? A place where it's easy for friends and family to interrupt you for a casual chat? Is the television on nearby and distracting you?

All right, now look at your writing surface and your chair. Make sure that they're adjusted at the proper height: your bent arms should form a loose "L" to reach the keyboard. Most regular chairs are much too low to use with a typical tabletop surface for typing. If you hunch over or have to reach up for the keyboard or mouse, you could end up with sore arms, wrists, shoulders, and so on—which can lead to serious repetitive-stress injuries such as pinched nerves, tendonitis, carpal tunnel syndrome, thoracic outlet syndrome, or cubital tunnel syndrome, to name a few.

I know from experience—my wife has had four arm surgeries to correct damage caused by an improper office setup from when she worked a full-time office job. Sit on a pillow if you have to, or install a keyboard shelf. Get yourself set up at the proper height. It will pay off big time in the long run—and you are in this writing thing for the long run, right?

Next, in order to make the most out of your office, consider your personal habits and schedules.

These will be different for each writer.

Some people write best at home in familiar surroundings, while others find the home environment too full of distractions like ringing phones and numerous little household tasks. Some writers find a coffee shop environment to be stimulating and inspirational with its constant comings and goings and background chatter, while others prefer to get away from distractions by renting a separate room to be used specifically as an office outside of the home.

For myself, I happen to be most productive when writing or editing with loud music playing; Rebecca, on the other hand, works best in total silence (yes, that means we have our offices on opposite ends of the house).

A side note: I use a set of noise-cancelling headphones while I travel. They are remarkably effective at shutting out the background hubbub of airports, train stations, and coffee shops—which lets me concentrate completely, even amidst the chaos. Try them. (I'm on an airplane editing this right now, with the headphones on.)

Now consider another thing: What time of day are your peak imagination and energy at their peak? Everyone has different cycles. I'm a morning person, and I get the most work done first thing in the day with fresh coffee running through my bloodstream. Rebecca is a lot slower to get moving and doesn't do much creative work until later in the day, but then she stays up well beyond the time when my sleepy brain is shutting down.

If you're a night person, try to arrange your writing time for late at night. If you're a morning person, get up a little earlier to do your creative work. Pay attention to your own rhythms.

As an experiment, try writing under different circumstances, at various times, and in a variety of places, then determine the best environment for you. Which collection of variables allowed you to produce the most words that day? You may be surprised what you learn about yourself.

Then, once you've figured out how and where you can be most productive, arrange your schedule and your office environment to accommodate that. Be proactive instead of reactive.

Writing Productivity Tip #9
Think Outside the Keyboard

All right, now that you've set up your perfect writing office, keep in mind that this is not the only way you can write. Your computer isn't the only tool you have.

Think outside the keyboard.

If you can learn different ways to write, in different places, at different times, with different tools—like a talented musician learning to play several instruments—then you can take advantage of just about any situation in which you find yourself. And you'll get pages of writing done, no matter where you are.

I have a desktop computer in my office, where I do most of my editing. I am just as comfortable working on my laptop whenever I'm away from home—in restaurants, at hotels, on airplanes. But it doesn't stop there.

Remember the old pad and pencil? For those times you find yourself alone in a coffee shop, or riding the bus, or sitting at a picnic table outdoors, you can jot down notes, outline a story, write a rough draft. By hand. It's worked for a lot of writers throughout history.

My wife and I once plotted and outlined an entire Star Wars "Junior Jedi Knights" trilogy in an Italian restaurant using crayons on the white butcher-paper tablecloth. Before leaving, we tore off the wide section of paper, folded it, and took it home with us as our "notes."

I prefer to do my initial writing with a handheld recorder. I love to go out hiking on beautiful trails and take inspiration from the scenery around me—with the added advantage that it gets me away from all the interruptions at home. If I really want to, I can even hike in places where there is no phone service. Writing by dictation lets me be productive during an already enjoyable outdoor activity.

Sometimes with the recorder I just talk myself through plot snags and let my imagination roam. I'll develop imaginary biographies for characters or histories for my fictional worlds. Most of the time, though, I dictate finished prose, from the first line of a chapter to the last. My productivity record (so far) has been composing 45 pages of finished prose in a single, very long, hike.

Speaking finished prose out loud into a voice recorder may feel awkward until you get used to the idea. Some writers couldn't quite get the hang of it; several told me they felt too self-conscious walking along and talking to themselves—but it's not so different from talking on a cell phone. Nowadays, we're all used to seeing people talking into thin air.

Any kind of writing is a learned skill and requires practice. You didn't type 200 words a minute the first time you touched a keyboard. "Typing" seems unnatural to a beginner—the keys are in a very strange order, but you get used to it and then pick up speed.

Same with dictation.

While this might not seem to be a writer's traditional technique, keep in mind that the story-teller's art has always been a spoken one. Revered shamans would tell tales around the campfire, legends of monsters in the darkness or heroes who killed the biggest mammoth. Homer did not write his epics down. What could be more natural than speaking your novel aloud before committing the words to a computer hard drive or an editor's red pencil?

Before I learned to carry my recorder along with me, I would inevitably come up with snatches of brilliant prose as I walked along far from home, and by the time I hurried back to my keyboard, I'd forgotten it. With practice, though, I now dictate finished text off the top of my head (which I still polish after the pages are transcribed).

The drawback with a recorder is that someone has to transcribe your words, which can be a tedious chore if you do it yourself. Numerous typing services are available to do this for a reasonable fee, and there's even voice-recognition software (although science fiction terms can make the learning curve rather steep). I currently use an Olympus DSS 7000 digital voice recorder, with the attendant software to download my audio files and email them to the typist.

Other people have developed their own unique alternatives to sitting-at-the-typewriter writing. Find some for yourself, see what your natural method for storytelling is.

Writing Productivity Tip #10
Get Inspired!

Every creative writing teacher repeats the classic axiom, "Write what you know."

Therefore, the more you *know*, the more you'll be able to write *about*.

Every experience, class, interesting acquaintance, or place you visit goes into your pantry of "ingredients" for new material. Part of your job as a writer is to collect these ingredients so you can use them to add color and veracity to your prose. So— learn new subjects, do new things, meet new people, see new places. You never know what flavors might combine to make a fabulous dish.

Strictly to broaden my knowledge-base of experiences over the years, I've taken a hot-air balloon ride, gone white-water rafting and mountain climbing, traveled to various cities and countries, been a guest backstage at rock concerts, attended a world-class symphony, taken tours of high-tech scientific research installations, gone aboard a giant aircraft carrier as well as cruise ships, been on the floor of the Pacific Stock Exchange, gone zip-lining and indoor skydiving, summited hundreds of mountain peaks, and toured behind the scenes at FBI Headquarters.

You'll be surprised how many doors open to someone who says "I'm a writer doing research."

Feeling less adventurous? Then do other things to get inspired. Read extensively in a wide variety of genres, research esoteric topics, take a class about a subject you know nothing about. Sign up for a ballroom dancing group, hang out with a model-rocketry club, go outside at night and learn the constellations. Watch documentaries at random. Go to a museum—especially an oddball one. Here in Colorado Springs, for example, we have the trolley museum, the Olympics museum, a mining museum, an insect museum, a fine arts museum, a pioneer museum, a figure skating museum, a money museum, an air and space museum, a ghost town museum, a figure skating museum, an antique billiard museum, and the Pro-Rodeo Hall of Fame.

But it doesn't have to be that formalized. In your daily life, open your eyes and observe what is around you. Every experience you have is filled with details you can absorb and use at some later time. Watch people. See what they do, observe how they act, listen to how they talk, try to understand who they are and make up biographies for them.

In short, exercise your creative muscles. Go outside your comfort zone. Stock up your mental pantry with ingredients so that you'll have a variety of interesting things to cook with.

Of all the things you see, do, and learn, you never know what might spark a story idea or an interesting character. Being inspired will add to the energy you can put into your writing.

Writing Productivity Tip #11
Know When to Stop

Science fiction master Robert Heinlein proposed a set of rules for writers, starting with "You must write" and then "You must finish what you write."

Yes, actually *finishing* is the key.

Endless polishing and editing and revising and polishing again and then rewriting and then editing does not make a story *perfect*—it just makes a story *endless*.

Some writers start out with a promising draft of a story, then they begin polishing ... and polishing ... and the story vanishes into a black hole of never-ending revisions. It's never good enough to send out, and so it never gets sent out, and so it never gets published.

Early in my professional career, I ran a monthly writers' workshop with a group of fellow novelists and short-story writers. One member brought in a new story to be critiqued. It was fairly good, and we suggested some improvements. He took it home, then brought in a revised version for the next month's meeting critique, and we again made our comments.

And he did the same thing for the next three months. Same story, draft after draft, meeting after meeting. After a certain point, there was no noticeable improvement. The story was stuck in an infinite loop. As far as I know, he never submitted it anywhere.

Mike Resnick, who has won more major awards than any other writer in the history of science fiction, once told me his philosophy of diminishing returns in editing. He can get a story 95% perfect (by his measurement) in several drafts, at which point he could either work for another month to nudge the story a percentage point or two better (subtle differences that few, if any, of his fans would notice), or he could spend the same amount of time and effort writing a whole new story. "Which would my fans rather have?"

Finish the story. Send it out. Then write another one.

Don't misunderstand: You can't turn in a sloppy manuscript, and each submission should be as good as you can make it, but there comes a point at which you aren't really improving, but just marching in place. Are you becoming obsessive about rewriting and polishing? Are you making cosmetic changes and circular edits that no longer improve the story?

Is it possible you're simply looking for excuses to put off finishing the manuscript? Avoiding sending it off to an editor somewhere?

It's done!

On to the next one.

❖

To recap:

1. Shut up and Write

2. Defy the Empty Page

3. Work on Different Projects at the Same Time

4. Dare to Be Bad (at First) ... Then Fix It

5. Use Every Minute

6. Set Goals for Yourself ... and Stick to Them

7. Know the Difference Between *WRITING* and *EDITING*

8. Create the Best Writing Environment for Yourself

9. Think Outside the Keyboard

10. Get Inspired!

11. Know When to Finish

CONCLUSION

A fast writer is not necessarily a bad writer any more than a slow writer is automatically a literary genius.

No matter what your writing speed, you have to find time to write in a hectic schedule with many conflicting priorities. When you do find time to write, make the most of that time and produce finished prose.

I hope these suggestions will help you increase your writing productivity. Some of the various ideas may not work for you—they don't all work for me, all the time—but they are techniques to help you think outside the box. Try something different and see if you find it effective.

The one absolute piece of writing advice is that authors are all different, and there's no *right* way to do it.

Okay, time's up. The book is over. Now get back to writing.

ABOUT THE AUTHOR

KEVIN J. ANDERSON has published 125 books, more than fifty of which have been national or international bestsellers. He has written numerous novels in the *Star Wars*, *X-Files*, and *Dune* universes, as well as a unique steampunk fantasy novel, *Clockwork Angels*, which is based on the new concept album by legendary rock group Rush. His original works include the *Saga of Seven Suns* series, the *Terra Incognita* fantasy trilogy, and his humorous horror series featuring Dan Shamble, Zombie PI. He has edited numerous anthologies, including the *Blood Lite* series, the *Five by Five* series, and *A Fantastic Holiday Season*. Anderson and his wife Rebecca Moesta are the publishers of WordFire Press.

OTHER WORDFIRE PRESS TITLES

Our list of other WordFire Press authors and titles is always growing. To find out more and to see our selection of titles, visit us at:

wordfirepress.com